YOU TRY PAA:
A LOVE SONG IN TRANSLATION

YOU TRY PAA

A LOVE SONG IN TRANSLATION

CYNTHIA ANN CAUL

Published by Cynthia Ann Caul

2020

ISBN: 978-0-578-71637-4 (paperback)
ISBN: 978-0-578-71638-1 (e-book)

Printed in the United States of America

First Printing, 2020
Published by Cynthia Ann Caul
www.cynthiaanncaul.com

PREFACE

· · · · · · · · · · · · · · · · ·

This work is many things to me. It is a celebration of humanity and resilience. It is a tool through which I critically examine community and international development, the Peace Corps, and my role in both of those institutions. It is an exploration of identity and what it means to be of a certain race, country, gender, or religion. Both in terms of how one perceives themselves and how they are perceived by others, as well as the broader implications that transcend these perceptions.

More pointedly, it is an exploration of my experiences as a white woman from the United States, my white-ness and my U.S American-ness, living in a rural community in Ghana, West Africa trying to "do good," but sometimes doing quite the opposite, or simply doing nothing at all.

I call it a love song, because I have so much love in my heart for Ofosu, my co-workers, students, friends who became family, and this period of my life. During these years in Ghana, I learned so much, and what I learned became such a foundational part of the person I am today.

My time in the Peace Corps was in so many ways a time of fulfillment and intellectual stimulation, but it was also a time of moral conflict. I have spent much of my life since my service trying to figure out what to do with the knowledge I acquired there.

I struggled with whether or not to publish this book, and consequently, have waited for over a decade to do so. I feared it might be an exploitation, taking the stories of others in order to share my own. Quite frankly, I sometimes fear my whole Peace Corps service may have been an exploitation. I learned so much more than I taught and received so much more than I could have ever given. This cannot be over-stated.

Ultimately, I decided to publish it, because I believe it is important for people like me, white people and citizens of the U.S. and "western" or "developed" world, to speak openly and candidly about our unearned privilege, power, and influence, in order to foster productive conversations about how we can bring about needed change. This publication is my attempt to start one of those conversations.

Cynthia Caul
June 13, 2020
Pittsburgh, Pennsylvania

ARRIVING HERE

How many times
I have tried
to transcribe
these stories.

I have put pen to paper,
to napkin, to the back of
my grocery list,
in journals,
on laptops,
on iPhone applications.

Scattered
like the thoughts
in my mind.

I steal words
to cobble together
meanings
from moments
I am still trying to understand.

And the more time that passes,
the less clarity prevails.

The more I speak,
the less sure I am
that I even say
anything at all.

YOU TRY PAA:
A LOVE SONG IN TRANSLATION

TABLE OF CONTENTS

••••••••••••••••••••

DEBORAH'S STORY

Deborah's is the story
that lines the
backs of my eyelids.

Even now, ten years later,
a week does not pass
that I do not read it there.

It is not my story,
but one of the greater injustices
is that I am the one telling it.

My telling will be inherently flawed.
I will forget things
and remember them wrong.
It will be Deborah's story,
but only as much
as it has become
a part of my own.

PART ONE: THE PLACE OF DEPARTURE

SEPTEMBER 29, 2008

We boarded
as the news struck
then ticked
across every screen
in the terminal
with a frenetic phosphorescence.

The crunching
and crushing
and crashing
of the stock market.

The seven hundred
and seventy-eight
point plunge.

The final boarding call
barely audible
above anchors
reading text
typed feverishly
into teleprompters.

But those of us listening
still heard it.
We boarded up
and left.

CALL TO PATRON SAINTS

Fa. Da. Fada. Fadafadafadafadafada,
Oh Father,
forgive me for I have sinned.
It has been eight years since my last confession.
The first German priests arrived here in 1847.

Vitus, Boniface, they're marching—
Stechschritting past cinder block classrooms
with thatch and tin roofs.
They're Saluto romanoing,
        Bellamy saluting,
                Hitlergrußing their flag.

And then, they Schuhplattler,
spinning circles at the center
of their school yard.
Celebrating independence.

⸏

George, their uniforms—
like little boy then girl scouts—
without patches, despite their
proficiency at tying knots,
cooking over fires, and
stitching garments.

Homobonus, their sewing machine
is for sale at Urban Artifacts.

Elizabeth, their oven is on
display at the Smithsonian.

Adelard, Martin of Tours, their cutlass
is tucked away in my tenth grade textbook:
Jungle Warfare and Machetes.
They use them to mow the lawn.

Isidore, help me to teach
computer science without computers:

I write W W W on the board.
As I turn,
they rise,
synchronized,
arms at their sides,
chant: *Wol Why Wehp!*
And down.
Back in their seats.

I swear. I know I shouldn't swear,
that charcoal iron sits next to
Abraham Lincoln's death bed on the
tenth street of the capital.

Michael, Gabriel, Raphael, they use it to iron
out the wrinkles in their Obruni Wao—
the clothes they've purchased
at the Dead White Man's Market.

OFOSU

I am lying on a rice sack
strung between two poles.
My body is wrapped
in two yards of cloth.
The rooster crows.
The sun rises.
I bathe beneath it with a
bucket of fresh rain water
guttered into
blue barrels by my
tin roof.

Over the four five-foot
walls of my bath house,
I steal glimpses of
sewing machines,
school books,
water pans, and
firewood perched atop the
heads of passersby.

I am home and
heart sick.
I am in love
with a life I think
I will never live.

I am immature and
underqualified.

I shouldn't be here,
but due to centuries
of privilege,
I am.

YAA PIGRI

We arrive in a clearing.
I have passed many times,
always missing the nuance
I see now:

A circle of trees surrounds us,
growing intricately
into archways and a canopy
that vaults a ceiling
high above us
as if a town hall.

Chiefs and elders are seated
in a line of plastic chairs
they brought from home,
carried in on the heads
of their children.

They speak hushed and hurried,
beyond my understanding—
except a few repeated sounds,
weaving a pattern
through their measured commotion.

They arrive at my name.

Yaa, because I came here,
was born in Ofosu,
on a Thursday.

Pigri, because another came before me called Kalenkyi.

Pigri: because she went away,
                    and came back.

BADU

My landlord's
eventual mantra
for me:

You try paa.
You try.

You try paa
[to wash your clothes by hand].

You try paa
[to fetch water from the borehole].

You try paa
[to start a fire],
[to pound fufuo],
[to sleep on a rice sack],
[to ride your bike],
[to carry a chair],
[to crack a peanut].

You try paa.
You try.

Anytime I do anything
he believes beyond
the wealth-induced
limitations
of my race.

SUSIE

Choking
allows you
to forego
certain
niceties.

The woman
who I've just met
washes one hand,
her right hand,
and holds me down
with the other,
dislodging the fish bone
in my throat
from the okra soup,
which I will never again
slurp straight from the bowl.

FINE

Here, fine is literally fine—
not a sardonic counter, but
                    good. Great.

The only allowable
response to *how are you?*

Everyone is always
fine.

I am fine too.

DEBORAH

Deborah erupted into my life,
barely three feet tall.
She was invasive,
standing before me,
with her chest and belly
lightly grazing
the fronts of my thighs,
shouting the name
of the only other white woman
she had known
by way of a greeting.

She shout-sang it,
that other woman's name,
almost taunting me,
but she meant no harm.

Akosua Kalenkyi!

Ah-ko-see-a Ka-len-chee!

Akosua Kalenkyi,
Akosua Kalenkyi,
Akosua Kalenkyi!

I shout-sang
her own name back.

Deborah!

De-bor-ah!

Deborah, Deborah, Deborah!

And so,
we forged our friendship.

HOMESICK

The hat,
the boots,
the boy.

The late night
diner milkshakes' touch
of something kept cold.

The inhabitant
of this body
with its wings tattooed
on the right thigh—

the last remnant
of a relationship
with a boy-god
who broke things off.

I've been unmoored,
grasping for the scarf
I used to wear
around my neck.

I am lonely,
but never alone.
Always seen
and never known.

JUJU MAN

I know his house,
half a mile past the last structure
heading east
on the road to Nkwanta,
seen the smoke
from his fire
rising in the air.

I know the people who go to him,
but I don't know when
and I don't know why
until after—after
the house is stolen,
or the poison's taken,
or the snake bites,
or the sun fails to rise,
or he plans to take
Vera as his virgin bride.

I know all of these things,
but only after.

MAWUSI

On Friday nights
she'd come for *kinters*.

We'd paint the nails
of our left hands,
so we could still eat with our right.

She'd savor it for two days
before scraping it off for school.

FRIENDING

Friending
is what a boy
is doing to a girl
is doing to a man
is doing to a woman
when they see each other
without being seen,

but even
the unseen is seen
by someone here.

SAME MOTHER, SAME FATHER

Everyone is a brother or sister,
unless they're a mother or father.

A close friend, *M'adamfo paa,*
is your brother, *ɔnuabarima.*

The woman who dashes me
stew for my rice is my mother.
Maame, meduase.

The stranger who gives me way
on the tro is my sister.
Gaffara, m' ɔnuabaa.

All are family; no common blood
unless otherwise noted.

Ma ɔnuabaa: my sister—

maame baako na papa baako:
same mother, same father.

SLOWLY, OVER TIME

We never conversed beyond the basic salutations
I had memorized,
which, to me, made Deborah's behavior
indistinguishable from that of her peers.

I wasn't sure exactly what
her father meant when he told me she was *not normal*.
That she could not *think right*.

The extent of his English,
and my limited Lapuupuu
offered no further clues.

Another of countless puzzles
I am now accustomed to.

I learn things slowly,
connecting experiences to
fragmented phrases heard previously,
piecing them together over time.

And that is how it happened with Deborah.
How I pieced together her father's words
with her being *a witch*
with her *grandmother made her one*
with her seizing on the concrete floor of her compound.

That is how I learned she had epilepsy.

THE OTHER PLACE

The other place is falling,
memories slipping out of reach.

I sometimes see my mother
while I'm dreaming,
but she's just about to leave.

~

But then a neighbor passes
in his snowsuit
on the way to
weed his farm.

~

Or there's Susie
in a red polo
with Ronald's golden arches
on its sleeve
and *Brad*
embroidered
on its breast.

~

I spot the insignia
of a 1992 Penguin's jersey
half a mile away.

~

Anachronistic flashes
breaking through the fog,
boiling nostalgia
bubbling over from
the other place

still here.

SEASONALITY

After the rains,
comes the harvest.
After the harvest,
come the long, lively nights
filled with sounds
of humming generators
fueling cell phones and tvs
and sports commentators
narrating each toe kick,
back heel, yellow card,
and goal.

And jams that snake
through the houses
rising up through the air
and lingering until every body
that came out
or stayed home to dance
in the comfort of their compound
was soaked with sweat.

We named the babies
and honored the dead.
We ate pristine bowls
of fufuo, meat, and rice.

And then the silence
would set in again,
and we'd retire to our rooms,
live by the starlight,
and work until the rains,
and then the harvest came again.

FULL MOON

When the earth circles
the sun and is circled by
its moon in such a way
that those of us bound to it
become fully-illuminated reflections,

Badu, observing the hand
he can see in front of his face tonight,
turns to me to say *natural electricity.*

JUKE

One of the students
gave me a kitten,
who I called Juke,
like the box,
which is what she came in
on the back of his bike from Nkwanta.

I kept her in my room
to my neighbors' consternation.

There's death in the room, they warned,
and they were right.

One day, Mawusi left Juke out
while I was away at market.

Overtaken by dogs,
Juke survived
just long enough to find her way home
and greet death in my room.

PART TWO: THE MIDDLE PLACE

······················

JANUARY 4, 2009

Today someone told me:
sometimes we think
you people are our ancestors
coming back to help us.

~

Perhaps.
In a sense.

In the sense
that we've all come
from somewhere:

from Adam,
from Eve,
from Sarah,
from Hagar.

from the bowels
of an arc
that paired us
and saved us
at sea.

ESI'S ROLL CALL

They sing songs with
words I do not know,
but they are crying,
so I understand.

The students march in neat rows,
uniformed for classes,
but walking away from the schoolyard
on the town's single road.

I follow them to the funeral.
A girl—seven years, a baby—
is laid out on the floor
of her three-room house
with coins laid over her closed eyelids
and her belly round and hard.

Killed with no weapon
by an enemy of her father
and his juju.

In this town so small
with its houses so close
and everyone always within earshot,
he somehow managed
to find her alone.

She told us after
her father sacrificed three chickens before the priest.

She told us after
two days of not wanting to live,
two days of not wanting to die.

She woke up and told us:
He did it. He put it in the food.

Now, her teacher stands before his students:

Amadu, Fuseini.
Present, sir.

Bekilen, Abraham.
Sir, present.

Bekilen, Kofi
Present.

Mdena, Esi…
Mdena, Esi…
Mdena, Esi…

He calls her name three times
and will not call it again.

FARM

Day breaks
and the migration begins.

Some go east and west,
along the main road.

Others disappear into the tall grasses
growing north and south.

Everyone in different directions,
but heading to the same place—

farm.

I remain.
One of few ghosts
left to while away
twelve hours of day
before they return again.

APPRENTICE

The agreement was typewritten in town,
signed, fingerprinted, and sealed
for a small fee and
two bottles of beer,
Fanta, and Coke.

Susie's my master now.
She teaches me to sew
dresses and skirts
and school uniforms.

Top and down,
she says—
mustard and brown.

THE ACCIDENT

He approaches us
with his hand
arranged in the shape
of a gun—
two fingers and his pinkie
curved beneath his outstretched
finger and thumb,
which he has tucked
into the back
of his waistband.

He threatens to shoot me
before using the same hand
to pull me down
by the center panel of my bra.

As he grabs my purse,
he strikes the crest
of my cheekbone,
leaving the
faintest bruise.

He takes everything
I have, but I know
he doesn't mean to
hit me in the face.

MAYBE KWASI

Maybe he was born on a Sunday.

Maybe, if we had met in the daylight
at the market,
he would have greeted me and smiled.

But it was already dark by the time of the accident,
and too much had come between us by then.

ELEVATOR EYES

He takes me in,
Lifting his eyes,
then lowering them.

I greet him quickly
and too quietly
for his liking.

Displeasure rises
in his throat,
and today I am unable
to let it slip
through my ears
unatoned for.

I shout back,
gesturing with my left hand.

You are a slave trader.
You carried my fathers
out of this place in chains.
You are only here now
to perpetuate the onslaught.

I use his ignorance
of my origin as a shield
to deflect his accusations,
but he is right,
so it is irrelevant anyhow.

I am white.
That is what he is talking about.

ELEVATOR EYES REVISITED

Two weeks later,
we apologize,
and he playfully
asks me to marry him.
This time I ignore the rise
and fall of his eyes.

I am a woman.
That is what he is talking about now.

LOVE LOST

I met him on the beach near the Ivoirienne border,
five tros and several hours from Ofosu.
Several hours more during rainy season.

He was reading a book in French,
and I asked him to translate the title.

He came to see me a month after that,
and I him the next.

When we fought,
which was often,
he'd use *rastafari*
as a verb to calm me down.
It never did.

He always seemed placeless,
and I know now that he was.

I was one of others
he was friending,
hoping one of us
would take him away.

ESI'S SISTER:
SAME MOTHER, SAME FATHER

I find Abigail crumpled
over Esi on the floor
wailing.

Through the hymns,
through the service,
through the roll-call,
she remains

until they carry
her baby sister
out from under her,
place her in the hand-carved casket,
perch her upon their shoulders,
and take her on her way.

Abigail follows, wailing.

ABIGAIL

Abigail who is fiercely intelligent,
but makes nothing of it.

Abigail who goes to school,
but will not finish it.

Abigail who is a girl,
but this is not the reason why.

Abigail who is a child
of her mother and father
who know no promises
accompany an education,
who know the very system
is just one implemented
for their exploitation,

and *that* is the
reason why.

Abigail who boils over today
and every day in anger.

Abigail who only looks at me
out of the sides of her eyes.

Peace be with you, Abigail.
Anger stay with you, Abigail.
Even if I can only be the object of it.

TOO SLOWLY, TOO MUCH TIME

Deborah lay
on that floor
for two days
surrounded by promises
perpetually broken
by fathers and uncles,
always leaving
or leaving soon,
but never left.

She would no longer walk or talk
when she came home from the hospital.

But she would scream,
shrill and long-winded
through the sun
and the moonlight.

WHITE SAVIORS

The spiritual descendants
of those first German priests
still here building churches,
for "saving souls."

They stop when they see me,
a flash of pink flesh in their side window,
then rear-view mirror.

They U-turn
their way up to the shop
where I sit on a wooden stool
sewing dresses with a
hand-spun machine.

They all ask the same questions,
wear the same shock,
drive the same dark and tinted SUVs.

They all buy the same candy
for the kids
before they go.

Maintaining the archetype.
Taking us in like a road-side attraction.

WRONG ANSWERS

Sixteen ten-foot holes surrounded by cement
topped with tin

Sixteen pipes
Sixteen nets to keep the flies from getting in

Sixteen latrines to keep the high tides clean
as they wash through the kitchens of the compounds

Sixteen
turned to fourteen
turned to twelve
before the rain,

washing through the fields and the bushes,
through the compounds and the kitchens,

etches all the same wrinkles once again.

VILLAGER

is a word Susie uses
to remind me that we
are of different places
when she does something
that she thinks someone from the other place
would never do.

The other place where she knows water flows,
flushing toilets beneath electric light bulbs
left lit any time of night.
Where she believes people no longer require
education about using that water
to wash their dirty hands.

She's flippant with her use of it,
willfully self-deprecating,
but it is hard for me
to laugh with her—
the butt of her own
derogatory joke.

PRAYER CAMP

They've taken Deborah
to pray the witch or what
out of her.

You can get anywhere
with enough questions,
so I go.

I alight at Dambai
and ask my way
through the market,
buying rice and beans
from the stalls as I pass.

I ask my way beyond the fringes of town
where I meet the camp
and the improvised shelter
in which Deborah lies
alongside her mother
who stays with her there.

No common language between us.
We exchange abbreviated greetings
and smiles, which I bestow with subliminal promises
to pray for Deborah and hope they understand.

MALARIA

I have travelled this road before,
made this trip in this body,
not this car,
but this body,
not this body lying on its back.

I have seen these grasses before
they were charred and growing in again,
seen this road before
these craters were carved,
now the dust can kick up again.

And it does.
Churned out by the tires
as they enter and exit
the kettles on this water-etched road,
fanning embers inside of me.
One hundred and six degrees seize me.
And I seize.

They read my mortality for days.
in my blood, in my eyes—
they stare in to see
if they can find me.
I try to find my words.
I try to find my lungs.
Instead, I find a song,
and I sing it.

BUILDING CHURCHES

When they come,
every head-pan is filled
with water walked to the work site.

Every sack that ever held cement
is flattened and stacked by the side.

Each one is counted
to compensate the labor.

Then they lure a congregation
with Cokes and candy
into their fresh fabrication on Sunday—
predestined to sit empty
every Lord's day after.

DREAMS

The compound is empty this growing season.

Badu has taken the family to farm,
carrying the harvest to Accra
before bringing them home again.
The children missing most of the school year.

Because of money, he says.
If he gets money, he'll build a church.
That is the best business, he says.
Everyone who builds a church knows money.

SACRIFICES

I passed them on the way home.

The evangelical pastor
and his father,
church elder,
making an offering.

Two chickens bled out
on their forefather's grave.

Bartering for the
protection of their
other god.

The one that
doesn't deal
in cash.

UNOBLIGING DEATH

Elders came to scare
the death from her,
digging a grave
and placing her inside of it.

But Deborah stared
death squarely in the eye
and dared it
with each curdling scream
to suffocate her slowly
beneath the earth already
shovelled atop her head.

Death did not oblige her that day,
but left her two more years.

She was just barely six years old,
and I was already gone.

PART THREE: THE PLACE OF RETURN

PART THREE: THE FACE OF DEATH

DECEMBER 13, 2010

I looked back from the first step.

Everything going with me
already hoisted atop the tro.

I rubbed the worry stone
in my right pocket
and tried to memorize their faces,
how the station looked at dawn,
the smell of morning fires kindling.

I'd be in Nkwanta by breakfast,
Accra by the time
they returned home from farm.

And by the day after next
I'd be in the other place,
sitting on the couch
in my parent's house
in Pittsburgh
on the other end
of a worm hole
through which I'd never
find my way back.

ESI'S OTHER SISTER:
SAME MOTHER, SAME FATHER

Vera was the heroine
in a play the students wrote.

Vera was the heroine,
was the young girl,
who persisted at school
and resisted the marriage
with her words.

But tonight, it is a brother,
different mother-different father,
who smuggles her
into the bed
of a yam truck
on its way
to Nkwanta.

Tonight, it is an aunt,
in whose footsteps she follows,
who will receive her there.

Tonight, it is Vera's will
not Vera's words
that will save her.

She does not use words
at all.

Not to me.
Not to Abigail.
No.

Vera offers
no words
to anyone
at all.

Instead, we will wake tomorrow,
and find she has already gone.

HER OWN WAY

Abigail who found her own way out of trokosi
by friending the headmaster.

Abigail who is a girl.

Now that *is* the reason why.

LOVE FOUND

Meeting someone
for the first time
who you've known
for a lifetime

feels like searching
and finding
the perfect word
on the tip
of your tongue.

feels like knowing
a past before
the future happens.

feels like following
a path
you've already gone down.

feels like finally finding
quiet refuge from the
synchronized,
simultaneous
chatter.

WHEN PEOPLE DISAPPEAR

People are like smoke in the air.

You can see them until you can't.

And the fire has already burned out.

CATHEDRAL

Badu didn't build a church,
but he did come back from farm.
The children returned to school.

He did it in his own time.

Carved their destinies
out of the yam mounds
he piled high with fertile soil.

FACES

I see their faces
now lined up
across my screen.
Suggested people I may know,
but, truthfully, I do not.

At least not anymore
and also maybe never.

I message them anyway: *how are you?*
They all respond: *I am fine. And You?*

EZEKIAL

Susie called me
to name her baby,
one year after I left.

I gave her
a Konkomba and
a Christian name,
but the former did not take.

I trust a god
of any language
will still strengthen him.

WORDS

My ignorance of words,
or them of me,
makes us say too much
or not enough
or not exactly what was meant to be.

We dance around each other,
sometimes violent and fraught,
until one of us concedes: *yes,*
this is what we mean.

Only to change our minds the next day, reversing
the commas,
the line breaks,
the punctuation.

Moving words back and forth again
for ten years
and fifty poems
that piece together the
napkins and
iNotes and
grocery receipts.

Finding the meanings, then changing them,
then finding and changing them again.

MAY IT BE A LOVE SONG

May it be a love song
filled with words
I couldn't say
in the language
of a community,
not a village,
on the cusp of extinction
and its people,
not its villagers,
who are living,
not waiting,
for the other place.

EPILOGUE

....

A WITCH'S LAST WORDS

I can tell by her skin
she has money.

She came here from somewhere,
and the money she used to get here,
could pay my way to the hospital eighty-eight times.

I am tucked in this room,
trapped by my limbs
lain on this floor.

I breathe lightly for two days,
while my father waits outside
for me to die. I don't.
They all wish I had—

except the one with the money.
She thinks everything should live.
And she blames my father,
and he blames the witches,
and they dig me my grave.

They put me inside of it,
but I keep on breathing
and others, with that skin,
come with their cameras

to make me a martyr
for women,

but not
for witches.

www.ingramcontent.com/pod-product-compliance
Lightning Source LLC
Chambersburg PA
CBHW031539040426
42445CB00010B/616